Spit & Hiss
Mike Watts

To my brother, Tony.

SPIT & Hiss
Mike Watts

All rights reserved. No part of this book may be reproduced, stored in a retrieval system or transmitted in any form or by any means electronic, mechanical, photocopying, recording or otherwise, without the prior permission of the publisher.

ISBN 978-1-9031105-7-7

First published by Wrecking Ball Press 2018.

Copyright Mike Watts

Cover design by atomluft.co.uk

All rights reserved.

Mike Watts is a writer from Hull. He is the author of
three previous collections of poetry:

Coming to a street near you
(Night Publishing)

Day and night in the damaged goods factory
(Burning Eye)

Jawbreaker
(Paul Gibson)

CONTENTS

Goodbye Brentwood	10
Down the Plug-Hole	12
Song for Whoever	14
New Room	15
September Song	16
Little Red Corvette	18
Job and Money Situation	19
Nothing But Love	20
Cock	21
When The Dark Clouds Come	22
Twenty Four Hours Fifty	24
Pig	25
Night of the Jackals	27
Paella	29
Westbourne	31
Direction	33
And I Think to Myself	34
Deep Breaths	35
Hey Ho, Let's Go	37
Friday	39
Mean Green	40
Running Away With Me	42
Ten Years	44
Color Climax	46
As Mental As	47
In Other News	49
Mr. Blue	51
This is Where I'm At	50

Wardens	54
Said the Drunk at the Races	56
Terra Firma	58
Me Again	59
Little Lad Lost	61
Now's the Time	62
Sorry	63
Ten to Midnight	65
Feedback	66
An Animal	67
Electric	69
Intoxicating	71
Not This Night	72
Salvage	74
Straight Back To It	76
A Tenner on That	78
Long Way From Home	79
Salthouse Haven	80
A Toast	81
Filthy	82
Signed Off	83
Fashion	85
Pudding	87
Fragment	89
Let The Good Times Roll	91
Back to Now	93
The Way	95

GOODBYE BRENTWOOD

Back then
it seemed the right move,
but in reality we were simply swapping
one battleground for another, and, eventually,
after one skirmish too many, we fell.

And yet, despite the loss of everything we had,
everything we used to be, she recovered,
re-married, learned to smile again.

I stayed put: wrote poetry, took pills,
punched holes in doors,
replayed my funeral over and over,
until one night, I thought, fuck it.

Melancholy is my only vice now,
and sometimes, when I'm alone,
I turn to it, share with it whatever it is
I'm drinking, and we'll sit at the window,
watch the traffic, the dog walkers,
relax in a peace I thought long since gone.

A favourite once said:
'It's not the place's fault'

And it's true,
you were nothing but bricks and mortar,
the rest was down to us.

So I'll say goodbye Brentwood,
It was quite a time, I fulfilled some incredible shit
down that terrace,

but I'm here now
and I'm glad.

DOWN THE PLUG-HOLE

Today I helped clear the house
of a woman,

a woman who,
at just thirty nine,

despite the beatings,
the warnings,
the numerous efforts to
throw him out,

was finally murdered by
super-strength
and the rest of his violent crew.

The place was a ransacked hole
of cat stink.

After several hours
of clearing cupboards,
bagging empties,
sweeping through the
rot and shit,

her mam said to take anything
I could use.

I'm home now,
beneath the shower,
hair a squeak

of silken shine,
rinsing it all away;

the shampoo,
the body wash,

the mumbling sadness
of that broken mother

and her determined search for a carrier
to put them in.

SONG FOR WHOEVER

Unusually for me, I skipped dessert,
stuffed as I was on all the previous.

Necking the last of the Cobra, we settled the bill,
stretched into our jackets, stepped back into the same,
wet, shitty evening we'd scurried out of an hour or so earlier.

Still howling over an incident in maths four decades ago,
we shivered into the 'Haworth'
joined the throng of money wavers, three-deep around us,
as a guitar yelped suddenly, and soft female voice sent lyrics
to the hips and shoulders of every hopeful leaning to be served.

Soon we were seated, clicking fingers to 'Beautiful South'
    numbers
as bodies jigged about the place; then I was up, launched into it
by a Cleopatra-eyed pint drinker, black-tipped fingers
pumping our arms as we screamed the chorus.

In between mouthfuls, I broke free, made it to the bar,
drenched from the swinging, swirling, sweet-cider kisses of a
    woman
wired to something brilliant.

Mimicking 'short' to my mate, he thumbed-up,
and back at the table, we returned to it, the dust and rubble,
the dead and gone, the ghosts and shadows of how it used to be.
And as a sudden snare hissed, guitar whinged, I lipped a curse,
lowered my rum, shrank to his elbow of Egyptian queen,
wiggling straight for me.

NEW ROOM

For too long
rooted there,
huge corduroy thigh
and all the unwelcome shade,
crappy reception.
I lay at your trunk,
dreading each autumn,
the hours of sweeping as you shed,
dead and dying,
an endless crunch of golden brown
I can never keep
on top of.

Well, now it's time
to be screamed and buzzed through,
a fortnight's wage
on a whirr of dust and powder,
to see you felled and butchered,
hauled away in thick cuts.

And tomorrow,
when cloud dismantles itself,
I shall sit there,
turned toward the glass,
and in rays of shocking light
welcome a square of sky
I never knew.

SEPTEMBER SONG

I'm busy with Amy,
a student of philosophy,
picking blackberries close
to the rail track.

She's young,
hates my music,
films and authors,
but every Sunday,
after lying to her parents,
wiggles free from her jeans
and climbs in beside me.

Some days,
when I pluck out another
rogue grey,
the gap between us sniggers,
and when we make love
I'm as careful as a miniaturist.

In the morning,
when first light pushes through
the curtains
and she's wrapped around me,
it feels wrong,
yet
they slap my back,
call me lucky bastard,
swear they'd give anything
to be in my shoes.

Every day
I wait for it to die,

but
she keeps coming back,

singing her shit songs,
twizzling my chest hair,
writhing beneath my sheets whilst,
ten minutes away,
her mother straightens hers.

It'll end soon enough;
eventually she'll open her eyes
and do the right thing,

but until then,
here we are,
myself and Amy,
harvesting the final fruits
of summer,
purple fingers interlocked
as we carry it back
to her dad's old Ford,

a surprise for her 21st
birthday.

LITTLE RED CORVETTE

She's finally quit,
the broken heart upstairs,

screaming AIDS and cancer on someone
called Shithead.

I've been up twice,
but she doesn't hear.

As well as anti-depressants,
she necks gin and cheap sherry.

Still, she's a lovely sort,
baked me a pie once.

Tomorrow's a ten hour shift.
I check my phone, five hours to go.

Now,
if I can just shake this song out my head ...

JOB AND MONEY SITUATION

After all necessities,
there was £18 left.

I needed a new iron.

British Heart Foundation
was just across
the road:

opening hours
10 until 4.30.

I threw my last slice of white
under the grill
and re-filled the kettle.

It was just after eleven;

no panic,
I had all day.

NOTHING BUT LOVE

Listen to them, the locker-room studs,
with their tales of girls and sex
fuelled by coke and Viagra.

These twenty-somethings
with their hair and testosterone,
having it all taken care of,

slaves to the chemical
in this modern and effortless age.

Tonight after a ten hour shift,
I'll pedal home, eat and wind down,
have a glass or two,
and later, if the mood's right,
slide easily into it,

with nothing but love
flowing through my veins.

COCK

What I should have said was:
Me, yeah I'm seeing someone, have been for a while now.
But I'd rather weld another rod to the mountain of metal
already bending my back.

You see, I don't want to be like most people,
but I am like most people, the warmth of what we have is never enough,
it's how it's always been, egos so voracious we consume ourselves.

Now, I'm standing here, bloated with guilt, with voice mails and texts
that speak of heart-break and emasculation.
Were I not a coward, I would finish this piss and make amends:
Listen, I'm sorry.

But I know what I am, who I am and I'll tell you exactly what I'll do,
weaker than the water arcing away from me,
I'll just shake this little bastard and go to bed.

WHEN THE DARK CLOUDS COME

From my white plastic chair
I watch him,
crouched like a toad,
turning soil at the base of a tree.

He lives in the flat above me
and likes to fish.

Beside him is a jar,
a container for the invertebrate he's
trowelling for.

He says fishing helps
whenever he's depressed

and when he describes it,

the scenery,
thermos and sandwiches,
the gentle silence,
I can see why.

When I feel down
I scrub the bathroom,
eat shit food,
watch pornography.

Today my head
is where it should be

and it seems my angling friend
has found his bait.

Hopefully,
on a hidden bank somewhere,
he'll find himself.

Right now,
here in my white plastic chair,
it's all good,

and that bleach,
the pizza and pastries,
those hundred and twenty seven million
internet sites
are always on hand,
just in case.

TWENTY FOUR HOURS FROM FIFTY

Wheeling around the Henry,
I'm thinking of Stanley,
Mongrel member of the family.

Street roaming, cock-driven,
father of dozens, wanting for nothing
but bitch and biscuits,
until the day he keeled over,
out on a walk with my mother.

He just fell,
gasped out some breaths
then all his water came
away from him

Phone swinging in my hand,
as I slid down the wall.

Ah, Stanley,
you little bastard.

Some days I thought I'd
never make it,
but look at me now,
sucking up crumbs in my boxers,
blessed with so much
I'm almost embarrassed,

as a smile breaks through
and the tears spill again.

PIG

And there's me,
laying down my fishcakes and paper,
being read my rights,
cuffed and lifted,

in full view of neighbours
Angelika and Katrina,
Slovakian spud-pickers
I'd been working on for months.

Then bootless, on a torn plastic mattress,
staring hard at fingertips,
stained and captured,

thinking of women,
of Mexico,

of golden beaches
where I would brown beautifully
and never go back.

Three hours later, clutching paper,
I'm out of there,
bailed in the rain,
rage cracking my bones as I plan
a counter-attack,

a series of calls
where I'll vomit back everything
I know.

Pray to the devils
of fire and needles that my revelations
will be more than enough

to bury the pig that
                              did this.

NIGHT OF THE JACKALS

Fabulously drunk,
I fell upon this woman talking to a van,

You alright love? I enquired.

Yeah me mate's just tekin' a slash,

hey Julie get yer knickers up quick
there's a queue here, she squawked.

A minute later we'd locked arms,
six puppet legs stumbling, screeching a medley
of classics all the way back to mine.

And soon enough there I was, the disco fool,
shirtless and spinning before a slavering duo
up for Christ knows what.

And just when I thought I'd cracked it,
a sudden shock of limbs,
slaps and shrieks as the coffee table tipped, glass exploded,
cheap cider glugged onto the carpet,

the pair of them, down and rolling,
twisting and ragging like sharks at blubber.

I stepped in,
but within seconds it switched;
a fury you'd expect on the terraces, a picket line,

a riot of fist and nail, knee and heel smashing me
senseless into a corner.

I came round in a pool of piss,
skin The Way of the Dragon,
scalp hot and raw,
phone and wallet, someplace else…

A week to the night and I'm back out there;
no eight pints, no double whiskies,
just me, prowling the bars, watching, waiting,
space set aside on my living-room wall,
for the hanging of the heads, of two big cats.

PAELLA

Pussy's promised cold beer and hot girls,
but it was food I wanted.

Mehmet's just two further down
served up the best Doner around,
so I shouldered my way in, ordered and waited.

Fifteen minutes later, back on the street,
I popped open the carton, dug in a fork,
busied myself with the contents as I made my way over to
Claire's place.

It was a warm July evening and things were easy;
I was working, hadn't gambled in weeks,
was having more success with women than ever before.

Claire was the latest, I'd just seen at a bar in town,
on a hen do with workmates, she was completely wasted,
I was happy to walk away, but not before she'd given me
the keys to her flat. I'd left a few things there,
razor, nasal trimmer and most importantly,
my Mediterranean cookbook.

I'd decided to lay off Claire for a while,
she was sweet enough, but her insistence on constantly
trying to push a finger into my hole during sex
was wearing thin,

despite my vocal, sometimes physical protests
(I would grab one of her ears and twist it)

she would argue - *"What's a matter wi'yer?
you blokes love it, it's where yer g-spot's at."*

After finishing the grub, I dumped the empty carton,
continued along, keen to be in and out,
keys returned and back home as soon as.

You see, I really needed to consult that book; Desiree,
a dancer with ginger hair was coming over Saturday
and I'd promised her paella.

WESTBOURNE

Shuffling around,
filling my lungs
with this new place,

exploring it
carefully,
trailing my fingers
across its skin,
testing its taps,
flushing its toilet.

It feels unusual,
frightening, almost.

A new relationship
needs time;
I must respect it,
break it in
gently,
be sympathetic
with my choices,
my fabrics,
the depth of my
colours.

As the weeks pass,
the joy and the
horror
of what I am
shall seep into it.

Let new noise,
let the scratch
and the shock
of my alley-cat
screams
bring fire and steel
to its walls,
to its long windows.

Let nothing
but good
visit me here.

DIRECTION

Watching the Koi,

I thought

how wonderful it must be
to just turn suddenly

and go a different way.

AND I THINK TO MYSELF

Police are appealing for information after an 82 year old
man was found robbed and beaten.

My feet stink because of these old trainers and
I can see my breath because the boiler's bust.

In Mexico,
A dozen heads have been fished out of a well.

I need painkillers and pasta.

Last week's triple rollover has finally been claimed;
the £14million prize was believed to have been won
by a builder from Surrey.

I've told everyone to forget about me this Christmas
because I can't afford to think about them.

After a dull start there will be prolonged and heavy rain.

It's almost 4 years to the day that Sam died.
She was pregnant with twins.
My mate Lewis was the father.

And now,
a classic from the wonderful Louis Armstrong…

DEEP BREATHS

Here I am,
a month later,
half a stone lighter.

Never saw that coming,
real sniper's bullet.

But everyday I feel
added to,
a little stronger.

And tomorrow
I'm meeting someone,

a guitar playing
bakery worker
who wants me to sing.

She's come at a good time
and
I think I'm ready.

When they leap in,
the images,
the unwanted thoughts,
take four deep breaths and
scatter them,

Is what you said I should do,

and you're right,
It's the only way.

HEY HO, LET'S GO

A blazing bank-holiday,
all-day bender
and me leathering cars
on a baking forecourt
whilst you bandits
crawled the Marina,
getting wrecked,

buzzing my phone
with beer and birds,
rubbing it in,
tormenting a soul
gutted not being there.

Cheers lads.

Was just after five when
the call came:

John's gone mate he's gone,
he's dead.

Me with a grin as wide as
the Humber,
not falling for them,
the stuttering sobs
as one voice then another ...

And soon it sank in.
No wind-up.
John was dead.

Countless lagers,
shots and ciders
and there he was,
pissed-up and pogoing his
Blitzkrieg Bop
onto an A63
that grabbed him,
threw him over its shoulder,
ending his and theirs
and some van-driver's day
with a bang.

We're all here now,
me and the lads,
waiting for him,
decked out in City flags,
up on the shoulders
of brothers and uncles
as we follow them in,

take our seats,

trickle smiley tears
to the belting tune that
finished him.

FRIDAY

Dark rum crackles over ice
as the buzz begins to build outside a bar
in downtown Manhattan.

But I'm not there, I'm here,
listening to the song and swear of shirtless scaffolders
as I shuffle in a queue for cash.

Sandwiched between pink punk and pregnant Pole,
culture posing everywhere
as I edge closer to the wall,

turn a card through fingers that have stacked and served all week.
And that machine, I'm drooling for it,
its skinny slit to suck on my plastic, spit out the Queen,

lift me as high as they are, those scaffolder boys,
because their noise is my noise,
two sleep-ins and enough coin to spin us round and round

until Monday morning's kidney punch jolts us,
un-glues our eyes, drags us back to the beginning
of another beautiful end, because that my friend,

is what it's all about.

MEAN GREEN

Invested in a juicer,
the latest model, that I use every day.

If it's green and growing,
it goes in.

I'm not mad with it,
not obsessed or preaching,
but the processed party's over.

Now it's micro-nutrients,
re-booting the system,
re-booting the life.

It's not easy;
I'm no hunter-gatherer,

my fodder came packaged,
tinned and frozen,
boxed and ready to go.

Not anymore.

And I've given instruction,
should I clutch my chest
one glorious summer,
pulling beets in my muddy boots:

Just toss me in a corner
beneath the roots
and rubbish,

let time enrich us,

then scatter,
rake and dig me in

and come the green of that
new crop,

whizz it round and round and round
and drink us down.

RUNNING AWAY WITH ME

It was the new girl opposite,
an attractive
E-cig and vaping specialist:

Did I have a corkscrew?

She looked incredible;

silken red dressing gown,
white towel wrapped high around
her head

I have somewhere, I said
come in.

As I rummaged amongst the cutlery,

she lifted herself onto my table,
peeled herself open,
began to circle her nipples and pussy.

Unzipping frantically,
I yanked her toward me,

sank myself,

gasped and buckled
as she bit into my shoulder.

I've had no woman in here for over
a year,
a hunger impacting on my everyday,

and now here she is,
arms folded,
standing soft and silent behind me,

as I continued to search,

hands, trembling,
chest, banging,

the most terrible foul
running wild in my head.

TEN YEARS

We were drinking them down,
gassing about the fantastic job he'd fallen into,
half a grand a week plastering on a new development
across the river.

He said they needed labourers,
fifty a day in the hand,
he was mates with the foreman,
he could get me in.

It was a freakish hot day in March and here I was,
having my beer bought, being offered work.

It was our third pint,
we emptied them together,
then he dropped me a twenty for same again.

As I got up, his phone went.

Back at the bar there wasn't much happening,
some guy studying a crossword,
two women fingering menus.
The landlady was called Shelley
it said so on a number plate screwed to the wall.

She pulled two Peroni and I carried them outside.

When I glanced over to our table,
he wasn't there.
I assumed he'd gone for a slash.

I put them down, took a sip of mine then lifted my face
to the sun.

A few minutes passed, I got up and went back inside.
There was no sign of him.
I looked in the bogs, the lounge,
even poked my head in the ladies.

I didn't have a phone, so I couldn't ring.
I went out onto the street, into a bookies,
a newsagent, he was nowhere.

I drank most of the beers, took a piss and left.

I hung onto his change for about three days.
That was in 2008,
and I haven't seen him since.

COLOR CLIMAX

Vintage stuff's best, flock wallpaper,
Tretchikoff hanging,

blonde in white platforms, orange skirt,
flicking through Blue Jeans, cross-legged on a red vinyl sofa.

Suddenly there's something skinny at the window,
tank-top, purple waistbands, carrying a ladder,
sponge and bucket.

Fast-forward: skirt above the waist, knickers on one ankle,
nicotine-fingers jabbing at tumbleweed,
tongues twirling like grappling worms.

It's almost believable, his big square specs,
spaghetti arms, her crooked teeth, spotty arse.
No piercings, no silicon or six-pack.

On dedicated sites I watch them peak and pull out
in total silence, never touch the volume,
puts me off.

AS MENTAL AS

Regulars at the same
off-licence,
we did the usual
nod,
smile,
that kind of stuff

and what with her juggling
a twelve-pack,
a loaded bag of bottles,

it was the right thing to do.

So, taking everything she had,
we carried on up the
avenue,
carrier clinking at my
thigh
as she hit me with:

Tina,
unemployed drink-driver,
like writing down my
dreams,
got a cat – Oscar.
Did you know Joey?
Tried to strangle me,
locked up now,
burglary.

Churning it out until,
finally,
we got there.

Accepting a can,
I leant the rest against the door,
warned her about taking it steady,
turned and left.

A hundred yards into it,
she shouted after me:

Don't forget,
write down your dreams,
an' I'll tell you
what they mean.

Raising the beer,
I continued on.

That night I dreamed that
whilst surfing a cloud to California
Richard Pryor
thumped me in the back and
I coughed up a huge
feathery egg.

If I remember,
next time I see her,
I'll mention it.

IN OTHER NEWS

There are those who'd like to spend
hundreds of millions
searching out aliens in deep space,

what a great idea

We can share their intelligence,
their science, their warp-speed

Be just like ET,
cute and friendly
our kids will love 'em.

And I'm sure they'll come in peace,
be germ-free,
have no desire to enslave or eat us.

Yes, bring it on,
It'll be fantastic,
They'll cure our cancers, our differences.

I mean, what could go wrong?
you know ,
when man does what man does best
and they go mental,

reduce our cities to ash, farm us like cattle
for food and footwear.

Yes, I'm reading about it now,
hundreds of millions searching out aliens
in deep space,

stupid bastards.

MR. BLUE

The party's over,
the last of the rum a flame in my throat.

I've dumped the cards, the banners,
the saggy scrotum party balloons,
remnants of a night that never took place.
Just me, drunk with The Revenant,
Captain Morgan, dips and a dish of crisps.

Now it's June,
and I'm pacing the place, straightening pictures,
drumming worktops, opening the fridge
to gawp at blueberries, eggs,
the last of the marge.

I'd turn to writing, but she's gone too.

Sunday 4:09pm,
I'm at rock-bottom and out of talk-time.
Somebody, anybody, please,
if you're out there, for fuck sake,
call me.

THIS IS WHERE I'M AT

Sometimes you've an idea
how a thing's going to go,
so, at the last second,
you decide against it

The other night, for instance,
sitting there,
phone in hand,
all ready to invite
a certain someone over,
I began to picture
the scenario:

the draining of my booze,
time strangled,
the hours hung and bled.

And we've all been there,

settled on someone's sofa,
gabbed out trivia,
gnawed at their evening
whilst they snatch at yawns,
will us to leave.

Quite often I hate,
with all my heart,
coming home to zero
after a ten hour stint,

but right now,
with coffee steaming,
chips browning,
the sun spotlighting dust
as I pull out a book
in the quiet of this
high and empty room,

I can honestly say,
for the first time in
a long time,

nothing at all.

WARDENS

Squinting beneath it,
bending
this way and that;

purple clouds and
strange horses
vomited into a
golden frame.
And this is art?

I scanned the room:

nothing but
a bored guide
picking her nails,
two girls
texting,
a guy
fencing a wasp.

Nipping into town
to buy a belt,
I turned into
this place,

floating about,
lost in it all,
unaware that
just three streets away,

those sneaky bastards;
                        they'd got me.

SAID THE DRUNK AT THE RACES

Grab a pencil,
put it all into words,
it'll take the edge off.

So I began with

being dangled from
a balcony
at five years old,

screaming after the van,
taking Rex
to be executed,

squaring up to a tormentor,
stabbing him
with a tin-opener,
chasing him across a
busy road,
cornering and
stabbing him again.

A thousand lines
of rotten memory

ending
with a truth
so flammable,

should it ever be seen,

I'll be finished in
this town
for good.

TERRA FIRMA

A chunk of September wide-eyed across the pond,
now I'm back

and my skin, California-brown,
cools to the touch of Yorkshire drizzle, as I pay the taxi,
lug my stuff up the path.

Back inside, I let it all drop, inhale my absence:
silken vines, insect dead, a hit of fust in every room.

But it's good to stand here, reflection in the mirror,
Granddaughter smiling from a shelf,
and see, through windows weathered and shat on,

a stretch of trees, wet concrete, some guy sucking a cigarette,
all the wonderful nothings I never thought I'd miss.

ME AGAIN

It's Sunday afternoon,
and I'm trying to piss
as she speaks from
the kitchen.

Time I've zipped-up,
wiped the seat,
she's picking mint
from a beaker on the sill,

the room a sauna of
bubbling veg
as she lifts a lid,
scatters it into the steam.

I apologise,
ask her to repeat.

Forget it, she says,
snatches her phone
and disappears.

I scrape out a chair and
sit down
to a glowing oven,
rattling pans,
a morning paper vomiting
sleaze.

I adore women,
this one
especially.

Months back,
life punched me into a corner,
held me there
with a boot to the throat.

Then she came,
with comfort and wisdom,
a gift from the gods of
something to live for.

But now this
malfunction,
plunging the day into
confusion,
with the spit and hiss
of a dinner
good for nothing but
the bin,

if she doesn't come back
and explain just
what the fucking hell it was
I did or didn't do.

LITTLE LAD LOST

Unzipped, down some dark Redondo alley,
by a cutie, falling for it, the accent, the stories,
the heir to a title, Gallagher brothers on my phone bullshit.

Her, skinny jeans, crouching for it, a second taste
of the UK poetry scene, as I shudder beneath a stink of words
so rotten you could smell them back home.

NOW'S THE TIME

Weight of it all
reduced me to rubble,
now I'm rebuilding.

If fulfilment were a thousand bricks
then I'm a small wall.

They weren't lying,
those that said I needed shaking,

but I was struggling.
and no doubt
when darkness becomes a comfort,
something's wrong.

Nonsense that's behind me now.

Every morning
there's a flash of teeth,
a ten minute silence,
a determination to keep on at it,
to battle and build

until the fitful sleep,
the flood-water panic,
the shit and shock of those stabbed at,
punctured years,

are all but piss down the pan
                   when I'm done.

SORRY

Two old dears are busying themselves
in the dim light of the shop. One, in a curly black wig,
is hanging beads from a hook.
Her colleague, bald with wishbone legs,
is straightening shoes on a shelf.

I'm shuffling about,
checking out nothing in particular.

We are in the teeth of winter,
temperatures plummeting,
there is no laughter, no colour.

The shop is warm and quiet.
A man is at the window,
he rubs at the glass with his forearm,
salutes as he scans the display:

Suited mannequins, jigsaws,
a small table with a vase and flowers.

He steps inside.
Blasts of ice-cold air ransack the place
as the door jingles shut behind him.

I'm fondling a mug,
when my phone whistles.

It's Kirk,
his Viagra dealer has drank himself to death,

do I know anybody?

The mug is commemorative,
a chipped and cracked Silver Jubilee
with glued-back handle.
I replace it carefully, decide to leave,
shudder slightly as I rejoin them,
the grey, the damp and the dying.

At the roadside,
the traffic is relentless.

I dig out my phone:

Hiya Kirk, sorry mate,,
I don't.

TEN TO MIDNIGHT

On it
for a pus-filled toe,
I think of them,

the women,

gentle and caring,
sneaky and clever,
beautiful and mad,

all enriching,
all scarring me in some way.

I lie back
and see them;
blow-drying hair,
mashing spuds,
reversing my car into bollards.

Alone on this big two-seater,
I pour and put them away,
remembering too
just how good it felt
when music and food really
meant something.

There is pain here,
but it'll pass,
soon as Wild Turkey
and the delicious whack of her kisses
sends me over.

FEEDBACK

If I'm honest,
I get maybe
A quarter-way in
then my mind jogs onto something else;

you know,

gravy granules,
air in my tyres,

that kind of thing.

Then,
before I know it,
I'm at the end of a page
without knowing
what the fuck it is
I've actually read.

That's how it is for me
with most of your stuff,
you know,
if I'm being honest, like.

I'm not saying it's shit or anything,
Christ no, but it's
like I say,

you know,

if I'm being honest.

AN ANIMAL

Standing at the sink
I see them,

the tops of trees,

swaying twigs in these
late March
mornings

where stalled clouds
fracture,
allowing slices of
perfect blue
to lift the mood of a city
where, once again,
someone's fallen to the knife.

Reaching for my phone,
I swipe an image of
Jawbreaker,
re-read a message
ending
devils face and four x's.

Damn right,
last night was
incredible.

Will we do it again?

Fuck yeah!

and absolutely

I am.

ELECTRIC

Pausing only to suck at
stale air,
I continue feverishly,
determined to see it through
as conditions worsen.

It's January,
iced and bitter,
and beyond the shroud of this
cotton furnace
breath hangs like cig-smoke
as I labour in hot
sticky darkness.

Sockless feet poking into
the freeze,
the weight of layers
heavy on my head,
everything against me
as muscles tighten and skin
begins to drench.

At last,
just seconds from surrender,
a gentle gasp,
sudden lifting of the hips,
a ripple of abdominal wall
as a spasm of
wet flesh hammers
against me.

Crawling up out of there,
I sit for a moment,
caress my jaw in
triumph,
lungs re-filling,
licks of cold air
tingling around me.

As pulses calm
and blood returns to where
it's needed,
I turn away,
shuffle back to the warmth
of fresh love

as she kisses my shoulder,
swears my tongue
is electric.

INTOXICATING

The crackling orange of burning bales
brought no end of chaos,
but it cemented my place in the gang.

And throughout that hot and turbulent summer,
I swallowed turpentine, bricked bus windows,
threw myself into every dare, endangering and damaging
as we smashed and stole our way across the estate.

Until, after a near-drowning and several good-hidings,
I resigned, searched out a new challenge,
found it in girls,

where I've been endangering and damaging myself
ever since.

NOT THIS NIGHT

It's impossible
to create anything,

so I shut down,
peer through the blinds,

watch them,

madder than moths,

bouncing round the inferno,
screaming,
sloshing their beer

to the boom of it,
an air-raid of dance,

rattling windows,
shaking walls,
waking babies.

And as dogs freak,
curtains twitch,
porch lights come on,

there is little else to do
but withdraw,

fall into bed
and weep for it,

the poem,

kicked and clubbed,

gang-raped and
left for dead.

SALVAGE

Losing stuff is a new habit;

yesterday
I lost a poem

penned on the morning
Of New Year's Day.

I can remember only
fragments:

A trail of broken glass and takeaway,

chunks of spew,

the aftermath of celebration
strewn down a street
where Christmas yawns in big bay
windows.

And as deep as I've dug,
sifted through and overturned,
that's all there is.

It's gouged out such a wound,

the loss of it,

like coming home
to find my front door kicked-in,

an observation,
a flash of cranial activity,
deleted somehow,

save for a few weak lines
and the title,

which is of no importance now.

STRAIGHT BACK TO IT

In those few seconds
when I'm not
scanning and bagging
cereals,

wafer thin ham
and trifles,

I notice them,

pouting on a rack in front
of me;

the soap-star beauties,
emulsion smile and
cleavage,
announcing engagements,
miscarriages,
two-timing footballer
boyfriends.

Shit to yawn through
at the
hairdressers,

at gun point,

whilst an anaesthetic
freezes your gums.

And of course
it's important,
whilst truths are being
distorted,
that we are distracted,

as I pick up a cucumber,

spin it between my fingers,

bleep it
through.

A TENNER ON THAT

Winning, that's the danger,
you think you've cracked it, got a system.

So you're back there,
no skill, just a sweat-on,
a drumming on the heart,
praying that the ball will whizz and roll
bobble and bounce onto whatever it is
you're afraid to look at.

Then it begins, the thinning of your pile,
and as it shrinks, the chase intensifies.

No chance, the rot is in, sucking it all back
and more, until there's nothing,
nothing but a semi-conscious stagger home,
incoherent mumblings, a string of innards
trailing from your arse.

A genius once said:

How I made it to fifty with the luck
Of the cursed, is a fucking miracle.

Think it was me.

LONG WAY FROM HOME

Unshaved and sitting here, quarter bottle of Bushmills,
chucking down thoughts as radio remembers.
But the guy, his laughter, his belting hits of '84,
have gotten in, dried-up my juices, boogied me elsewhere.

So I'm logging off, stretching out, fingers clamped behind my head,
with nothing doing 'cept this whisky,
and Frankie, welcoming me to the Pleasure Dome.

SALTHOUSE HAVEN

Washed and wiped and wheeled
from rooms of cotton buds,
shrivelled peaches,
forgotten faces fading
in frames.

A row of shrunken heads
abandoned there,
busy bathing kids,
calling dead spouses,
waving to brothers lost at Dunkirk.

Each morning
a struggle to unravel
as TV flashes its alien world
and meds dished out
like jelly tots.

Relics of black and white,
of shillings and pence,
blanketed in chairs,
awaiting clarity,
tram rides to work

and strange voices
from dark faces,

with spoons of
something soft.

A TOAST

Thought fuck it,
bounced down the stairs,
took a right for the short walk home,

and there, on the avenue,
beneath an ocean of moonlit twinkle,
it hit me, like a windfall,
like a consultant's all clear.

And in the shiver of those beautiful seconds,
I smiled it all away,
passed the fountain, the health centre,
pushed in the key to my new place knowing that
soon enough, I'd be here,

raising a cold one in the California sunshine,
to the best move I ever made.

FILTHY

Naked at this fridge,
my tongue a pegged-out chamois,
I tip the milk and
glug it down.

The previous hours are
running riot,

guts on spin
and nothing in
to sedate the lunatic
inside my skull,

and everywhere
empty cans,
Chilean red,
the stink of whatever it was we smashed in.

I hate them,
these wrecked mornings
when you leave me,
sick and naked
with nothing but love dried around
my shaft,

and a saucer
spilling
with the crumpled butts
of your habit.

SIGNED OFF

I thought
being back with it
I'd feel restored,

I mean,
it's been a
long time coming.

I've had to prise myself
from the bottle,
navigate the maze,
re-join the life I'd
crashed out of.

And though I detest the dull of it,
the shit money,
the late finishes,
it's good to have a purpose,
a payroll number.

Yesterday I was summoned
to the office,
dismantled
for a mistake I'd made.

I hated unemployment,
that demeaning,
crushing kick in the cock,
stripping me of worth,

but this,
this
front of the class
bare-arsed whipping
made me want to
wreck the room,
throw combinations,
set about them in my
shiny new boots.

Last night,
whilst draining tuna,
I blasted off for deep space,
watched it all shrink
as I roared away.

This morning,
there's drizzle at the
window

and soon
I'll fire-up the Citroen,
hit the traffic,
heart sunk to the socks
as I search for the detour,
the sign,

the anything
that's going to steer me
a million miles from this.

FASHION

At the back of this bus,
where graffiti boasts of bestiality
and a blade of some kind
has torn through the blue cloth,
I watch a guy
with small compact
apply eye liner.

He's young,
pink leather jacket,
black curly hair.

I bite down on a nail,
think for a second,
fill in the bottom half

… short tartan skirt,
hooped leggings,
yellow Doc Marts
with purple laces…

We stop at lights;

he turns his face slightly,
runs a finger down his cheek,
pouts his lips
before snapping shut his accessory
and re-settling.

I imagine my dad sitting beside me,
his need for a Bren gun,
for national service,
for the world to end now.

As we approach the town centre
he springs up
in skinny white jeans
and baseball boots.

Doc Martens they ain't,

but they go fantastic
with his jacket.

PUDDING

After a good go on the dinner-lady,
I drove over to a friend's house
in the hope of conquering
my arachnophobia.

A red-kneed tarantula.
Big as a kitten
and twice as soft, he said
as he lifted it out the tank.

When I regained consciousness
he was on all fours talking to
the back of a bookcase.

Trembling into my jacket,
I clawed at my keys
and staggered out of door.

Later that afternoon
he said it'd been a nightmare,
trying to coax the fucker out,
and that I was a big fanny.

Tomorrow I'm staying in,
shifting for no-one
except maybe the dinner lady.

Tarantula,
big as a kitten and
twice as soft,
except maybe for her.

FRAGMENT

Poor bastard.
Poor old bastard,

his antique bike,
its rusty spokes,
the dozen bags dangling
from its bars,

sandals,
jacket with no hood,
thin white hair
pasted to his skull,

caught in this,

clouds growling,
saturating,
slapping like slingshot,

day gone dark as night

and the noise,
the fury of it all.

Poor bastard.
Poor old bastard.

I could cry for him,

as the lights change
and I'm away again.

LET THE GOOD TIMES ROLL

It tickled me to read of the political candidate
claiming he'd been punched,

his sneaky mug dominating the cover of my local
rag.

He swore that he was attacked simply for posting his
party's propaganda;

turns out he was being economical with the facts
(as I expected).

The alleged man-mountain of an assailant claims he didn't
take a swing at all,

he merely objected to having unwanted junk posted
through
his letterbox

and attempted to return it by pushing back into the poster's
pocket.

The candidate assumed it would be good publicity if he
reported it,

so the local press sent out a team to capture HIS
version of events.

The paper has an on-line comments section that stirred-up
quite a debate.

Some said the guy was probably an unemployed thug,
whilst others defended him.

Personally, I think the political candidate is a weasel,
I think most of them are,

and in this town I think he got off pretty lightly,
considering his politics.

This crappy bull-shit no news story made front page
so obviously all is well.

Diminishing crime rate, zero unemployment
and the local economy booming.

Pour the cognac, pass the cigars,
at last we've cracked it!

BACK TO NOW

Dazzling, amongst the chandeliers and soft-shell crab,
she lowers her cutlery, re-folds a napkin,
reaches for the wine she recommended.

Here, it's all violin and gentle murmur,
as I turn slightly, raise an empty bottle,
attract the attention of a bun-haired waitress,
soon popping and pouring a delicate red.

This is fine dining and I'm dining fine with Debbie,
that former mess we tormented to fatness,
when punk rocked
and the summers were long and hot.

Looking at her now, re-sculpted,
toned and slender, it's like
fucking hell, Debbie, what went right?

And I grimace, shrivel almost,
hearing back the poisons we clubbed her with,
the shame of it a bone in my throat,
as I scramble for excuses.

Truth is, I should be on my knees,
we all should.

Dismantled by misfortune,
I learned many things as I pieced myself back together,
forgiveness being the one that finally
put me right.

And tonight, as she straightens her dress,
gives thanks for a wonderful evening,
I hope she's learned it, too.

THE WAY

Decades ago and in awe of my heroes, I'd conjure up this image:
attic room, electric fire, radio playing, cigarette smouldering,
a shelf groaning with collections, reviews, another novel eight chapters in,
and me, hunched over a keyboard, hammering out the word, pissed.

I thought it was the way, uncompromising, unshaven, spitting out the window,
raging at the walls, bullshitting my way into bras, a bastard, liked, loathed,
admired by everyone.

Sadly I was never that interesting, talented or rakish, though I did once
sit down to it with a bottle of cognac, cock-sure I'd deliver, it fell horribly short,
a piss-poor attempt at fingering out something special overshadowed only
by the skull-splitting shock of hangover.

Sober, nicotine-free, as un-rock and roll as it gets, my habit is always the same,
sitting as I am, laptop on my knee, wondering where to go with this flat,
anaemic piece of writing, tea at my feet, the tick of a clock behind me.